Success with
Colour for your Balcony

FRIEDRICH STRAUSS

Editor
JOANNA CHISHOLM

MEREHURST

Introduction

Contents

A kaleidoscope of easy-to-understand colour

Elegant, playful, romantic or even strident – a skilful choice of colours will give your balcony that desired aura. Friedrich Strauss, a master of effective design with plants, demonstrates with this plant guide some successful examples of plant arrangements in your favourite colours. For each colour he provides information on where it can best be employed and what effects you can obtain. In order to demonstrate which colour shades can be successfully combined, the author provides a brief introduction to colour. Here you will discover how to employ colour runs and colour accords and how to obtain interesting effects with complementary colours.

Detailed descriptions of the beautiful plants photographed by the author make the topic easier to follow. Learn some of the most innovative design tricks: how you can make a narrow balcony look wider with the right choice of colour; how to make a roomy patio more cosy; and how to create accents skilfully.

Assisted by this book you are guaranteed much pleasure and enjoyment planning and gardening with colour on your balcony and patio.

For maximum impact, colour choice is essential in a small space.

A skilful choice of contrasts.

A harmonious combination.

The author and photographer

Friedrich Strauss has gained a diploma in garden design. His knowledge and instinctive eye for plant arrangements are supplemented by his studies in art history and above all by many years of experience in the cultivation, care and design of his own flowering plants. His wonderful photographs are much in demand with international garden periodicals and well-known publishing houses.

The illustrator

Marlene Gemke studied graphic design at the Fachhochschule Wiesbaden and is now self-employed as a scientific graphic artist. She has produced illustrations for several other titles in the *Success with* series.

Important: Please read the Author's notes on p. 61 so that your enjoyment of creating colour designs with balcony flowers will not be spoiled.

A symphony of colour

Frequently there is only enough room to fit a few plants on your balcony. This means that the individual effect of each plant you choose will be that much greater than in a more crowded planting. The right combination of colours plays an important part. This chapter therefore explains how you can use Nature's paintbox to create a priceless treasure on your balcony once you understand the art of designing with flowers.

Above: The blue spire of the grape hyacinths livens up the pink and white daisies.
Left: This romantic scene is based on a successful composition of different shades and intensities of pink.

A symphony of colour

Colouring your environment

Everything around us – our clothes, the decor in our living rooms or the flowers on the balcony – is coloured. With all these fabrics, furniture, flowers and leaves we like to achieve a certain aura or create a particular effect. How this is done depends on whether you wish to be reserved or loud, strong or delicate, romantic or strident. Fortunately, to match your own personal preferences, there are corresponding flower and leaf colours, and their accompanying colour combinations are all available for your use. Once equipped with the knowledge of which effect you can obtain with which shade of colour, the door is wide open for designing with plants to suit your own tastes down to the smallest detail.

Colourful personalities

Every colour has its own particular character and will determine in its own way the atmosphere of its surroundings. Yellow flowers, for example, will lend a cheerful appearance to your balcony (see Yellow, p. 24). Flowers in shades of dark blue, on the other hand, will appear more serious and cool (see Blue, p. 38). When blue is combined with orange,

it gives a more brilliant and lively impression (see Contrasts, p. 11). It looks more elegant when planted with white, cooler when associated with green, more playful when put with red and yellow. These characteristics can be achieved with every colour for any desired effect. These effects although numerous are not entirely random, as they follow clear rules which can be followed quite easily with the help of a colour wheel, and which will supply the tools for your plans and designs (see Understanding colours, p. 8).

Composing with colours

The most beautiful plants are only really effective if they are combined with some skill. Not only are the right choice of colours and their combinations needed but also the right arrangement in order to give expression to your balcony or patio. We will show you how to arrange large and small plants properly, as well as erect and trailing ones. You will also learn about the principles of designing with plants (see Principles of design in practice, p. 18). Allow the many plant examples to stimulate you into putting the principles into practical use. Whether you are dealing with individual plant boxes or large groups of

container plants, hanging baskets, mini-ponds or decorative fruit or vegetables, the second chapter from p. 21 onwards will demonstrate the most beautiful arrangements, colour by colour, with exact descriptions for do-it-yourself.

What are colours?

Colours are nothing less than light of a certain wavelength. Every surface that has light shining on it will absorb part of the light, and the remainder will be reflected back. Depending on the consistency and material of the surface, some wavelengths are "swallowed up" and others are reflected back – this is what determines the shade of a colour. Some objects reflect the incoming light entirely and appear white to our eyes. Conversely, black surfaces do not reflect any light at all. Because of these exclusive qualities, black and white are not generally considered to be colours. Light can only be reflected if light is present. This is why hardly any colours can be distinguished in semi-darkness or shade. On page 16 you will be able to find out which colours are suitable for more shady positions or for balconies or patios that are intended to look their best mainly in the evening twilight.

This floral garland reveals the wealth of wonderful colours available for your designs.

Understanding colours

The character and effect of colours follow certain rules, and any plant design will become much easier once you have grasped these rules.

The colour wheel
Illustration 1

The best way to understand the connections between colours is to have a look at a colour wheel, where all the colours are brought together (see illustration 1), as in a rainbow.

The colour wheel in fact contains only the three primary colours – yellow, red and blue. All the other colours are combinations of these basic colours: orange is created by mixing yellow and red; violet is made from blue and red; and green from blue and yellow. Further colour mixtures can be created from the three primary colours – for example, red-orange. If you lay these colours alongside their combinations, you form a colour wheel (see illustration 1).

Brilliance

When designing with flowers, you should pay attention to the brilliance of the colours. Some colours can be perceived even at long distances, while others unfold their charm at closer quarters. The most brilliant of the colours is yellow, being the lightest colour of the colour wheel. Red too is visible at great distances. Violet on the other hand, as the darkest colour on the wheel, has much less brilliance.

A colour's surroundings also affect its brilliance: yellow flowers, for example, look light and radiant beside blue ones, yet look much darker alongside white flowers. Using the right combinations you can build this phenomenon into your designs (see Colour harmonies, p. 10).

Lightness

Depending on which wavelength light is being reflected by a plant, we can perceive varying shades of colour (see What are colours?, p. 6).

The appearance of a plant will also be determined by whether it is light or dark. Orange, for example, appears to be lighter than violet, and midnight-blue flowers are darker than lime-green leaves. The lighter colours usually appear to be more lightweight and cheerful, the darker ones have a more serious, heavy aura.

Opaqueness
Illustration 1

The opaqueness and the amount of saturation allow a colour to look lighter or darker. A shade of one colour may appear in full saturation, which means as a strong red or a deep blue. However it may also be lightened and perceived as a delicate pastel shade (see illustration 1).

1 A colour wheel: cool colours below, warm above.

This means that cinnabar- or vermilion-red can turn to a delicate shade of old rose, blue becomes sky-blue, and violet is lightened to a pale lilac shade.

The colour spectrum
Illustration 1

Often it is difficult to decide whether a flower is still orange-red or already cinnabar-red.
Saturated colours (see illustration 1, inner circle): 1 Indian yellow/egg-yolk yellow, 2 orange, 3 orange-red, 4 cinnabar-red, 5 maroon/purple, 6 violet, 7 blue-violet, 8 blue, 9 blue-green, 10 green, 11 yellow-green/lime-green, 12 yellow/gold yellow.
Pastel colours (see illustration 1, outer circle): 1 light yellow-orange, 2 apricot, 3 salmon, 4 old rose, 5 rose/mauve, 6 lilac, 7 lavender, 8 light blue, 9 turquoise, 10 pastel green, 11 light lime-green, 12 lemon-yellow.

Colour connections

All important rules for combining colours can be derived from the colour wheel (see Colour harmonies, p. 10).
Warm and cold: The colour wheel can be divided into two, with each half sharing a certain characteristic. The colours around the blue area of the colour wheel are perceived as cool (see illustration 1, lower half), while the colours around the yellow area appear warm (see illustration 1, upper half).
A colour run, or neighbouring colours, is the term used for a group of colours that lie side by side on the colour wheel (see illustration 2 above; Colour runs, p. 10).
Complementary colours are situated opposite each other on the wheel (see illustration 2 centre; Contrasts, p. 11).
A colour accord, or colour trio, is obtained if an equilateral triangle is laid across the colour wheel (see illustration 2 below; Colour accords, p. 11).

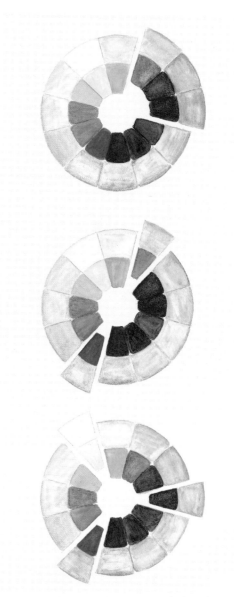

2 Neighbouring, complementary and trio colours.

A symphony of colour

Colour harmonies

Where you have more than one plant decorating a balcony or patio, you begin to create colour combinations. Stick to a simple rule of thumb in order to put together several colours harmoniously: combine only warm colours, that is those with a portion of yellow in them, or use only cool colours, that is those with a portion of blue (see Understanding colours, p. 8). Colours from the same "temperature" range will always harmonize well, even as pastel shades. In the case of shades of red or green, you will soon learn to distinguish whether they belong to the warmer or cooler part of the spectrum.

As well as this rule of thumb, there are also a few "classic" principles of colour combinations. However in order to achieve certain effects, people occasionally disregard the rule about combining only cool or warm shades.

Different shades of the same colour

Both very effective and simple is a design using flowers of just one colour. You will achieve enough variety with a range of growth habits and different typoo of flowers and leaves (see Principles of design in

A floral composition in red.

A colour run in pastel shades.

A colour accord.

practice, p. 18). For example, if you combine the well-structured flower of a red *Dahlia* with the large-petalled flower of the *Petunia* you will create an intriguing image (see photo top left). In a broader sense you can also use the word monochrome to characterize the combination of one colour shade with different nuances of opaqueness (see Understanding colours, p. 8). For an effective plant design in one colour, the chosen flower colour should be clearly evident. The green colour of the foliage will always form part of the picture when working with just one colour. Green opens up the image but should only dominate as a colour whenever you have chosen green as the main colour of your design (see Green, p. 42).

Colour runs

Colours that lie next to each other on the colour wheel are very similar (see illustration 2, p. 9) so they can be arranged in very balanced combinations. A colour run could, for example, comprise orange, orange-red and red, or flowers in neighbouring pastel colours oould be grouped together in a run (see photo, centre left). The safest way to create a harmonious colour run is by choosing colours only from the warm part of the spectrum – or from the cooler part.

Colour accords

Select plants from a colour accord, or trio, for a lively yet not randomly colourful design. Here too you can get guidance from the colour wheel (see illustration 2, p. 9): the corners of an equilateral triangle laid across the colour wheel will highlight a colour accord. The three primary colours (red, blue and yellow) form such a trio (see photo, p. 10 bottom). All other colours should be united in a similar harmonious accord, no matter whether you have decided on green, violet and orange colour mixes, or whether you prefer the finer, in-between colours, for example red-orange, blue-violet and yellow-green. A colour accord will never contain any strong contrasts and never appear harsh.

Contrasts

Colours that appear opposite each other on the colour wheel have nothing in common (see illustration 2, p. 9). They always belong to different parts of the spectrum. Complementary colours are

Complementary yellow and violet.

Complementary blue and orange.

Complementary red and green.

the proverbial opposites that attract and complement each other. The primary colours become complementary pairs by mixing together two of the three colours, resulting in: yellow and (the blue–red mix of) violet; blue and (the yellow–red mix of) orange; red and (the yellow–blue mix of) green (see photos, p. 11). The yellow–violet pair also forms the greatest light and dark contrast of all the colours. A combination of complementary colours is always full of contrast. Its effect is very strong if you have almost equal parts of the two opposite colours. If you use a complementary colour in small quantities in an otherwise monochrome design, the main colour will enjoy apparently stronger brilliance. You can create a similar effect if you place a "splash" of colour within a colour run, where the splash is a colour complementary to one of those in the colour run. This makes every other colour of the run appear stronger.

My tip: This little experiment demonstrates quite clearly the complementary effect. Look at a monochrome image for 20 about seconds, then close your eyes. The visual centre of your brain will immediately conjure up the corresponding complementary colour before your closed eyes.

A symphony of colour

The effect of colours

Many people have a favourite colour. Some prefer cornflower-blue for their clothing or their home decor, others feel drawn almost magically to anything orange-yellow. Mostly our preferences for a certain colour are based on the notion that the colour will awaken pleasant moods or memories.

A colour may trigger similar associations in very different people. For many people, for example, red triggers a vision of a field of swaying poppies or a picture of a ripe, crisp apple. Lush green fields and rustling leaves in forests appear before the inner eye when the colour green is mentioned.

Just like the sound of music, the sight of certain colours can influence thoughts and feelings. This fact becomes even clearer to us when we have had to make do without the sight of strong colours for a long time, for example after the long, dull winter months. The appearance of the first flowers in the softened spring soil cheers us up and awakens our spirits after a winter sleep. Every colour when present in certain quantities has a very definite and special effect on the observer:

● Yellow, red and mixtures of these colours have a

Introducing changes without the need for construction work

● Greater depth: Blue (see p. 38) and white (see p. 40) suggest spatial depth, especially if they are placed in the background.
● Visually enlarging an area: White, blue, or pink combined with white can seemingly enlarge a small balcony or what appears to be a narrow patio (see Pink, p. 32).
● Visually shrinking an area: If you find your balcony or patio uncomfortably large or believe that more clearly defined boundaries would enhance the shape, introduce shades of yellow. Yellow and orange ensure a more secure atmosphere (see Yellow and orange, p. 24).
● Eye-catcher: Yellow will supply your design with more than just an external

appearance of firmness. It is also eminently suited to drawing the eye to a particularly attractive centrepiece. The great brilliance of yellow means this colour is noticed by an observer even from a great distance. Red too lends itself to creating accents in out-of-the-way spots as it can bridge larger distances (see Red, p. 28).
● Effectiveness at a distance: If you want your balcony to be visible from the path or road below, select red, bright pink and yellow flowers because these colours are the best at attracting attention.
● For greater effect close to the observer: More delicate pastel shades of colour have only a limited brilliance. They are therefore best suited to designs near a sitting corner or if there is little space available for your plan.

stimulating and activating effect but, while yellow tends to lift the mood (see p. 24), the more passionate red may also be felt to be aggressive if there is an abundance of it (see p. 28). Orange possesses both something of the cheering-up character of yellow as well as some of the temperament of red but mainly exudes an

impression of warmth.
● Contrasting colours create considerable tension (see Contrasts, p. 11).
● For a more cooling effect choose blue and white. Both colours appear refreshing and calm. Blue tends to be more melancholy and may even be perceived as heavy or dull (see p. 38). White, on the

Vivid patterns can be formed by combining very small and very large flowers.

other hand, radiates purity and elegance (see p. 40).

● A very relaxing, calming effect can be created using a warm shade of green in a design (see p. 42). To conjure up a quiet, pleasantly harmonious atmosphere on your balcony, why not combine several colours from a colour run, which does not emphasize contrasts (see Colour runs, p. 10).

Designing spaces

Just as you can create moods with colours, it is also possible, through a targeted use of the right colours selected entirely according to your own taste, to create an impression of cosy comfort or generous spaciousness (see box). The most varied spatial effects can be achieved not only with the colours of flowers and other parts of plants but also with containers, furniture and other decorative elements. In addition to the design elements you choose yourself, it is also important to consider in your plans those elements over which you may have no control, such as the surroundings of the balcony or patio. What colours are the walls, the railings, neighbouring houses, balconies? Is there a garden attached? Your colour design will be even more effective if you are able to include these factors in your planning.

A symphony of colour

Enriching the palette of colours

● Violet-blue berries are displayed by the beauty berry (*Callicarpa*) and juniper (*Juniperus*) (see Blue, p. 38).

● Red berries are carried after the flowers on *Skimmia japonica*, *Pernettya*, firethorn (*Pyracantha*), *Cotoneaster*, *Berberis* and ornamental apple (*Malus*) (see Red, p. 28).

● Red foliage develops on sumach (*Rhus typhina*), Virginia creeper (*Parthenocissus*), maple (*Acer*) and sweet gum (*Liquidambar*) in the autumn. Bugle (*Ajuga reptans*) displays dark red or orangy dark red, variegated leaves all year round (see Red, p. 28).

● The orange-coloured fruits of ground cherry (*Physalis*) can even be used as Christmas decorations (see Yellow and orange, p. 24).

● Yellow fruit on ornamental quince are produced after the red or pink flowers have been fertilized (see Yellow and orange, p. 24; Pink, p. 32).

● Yellow- and white-patterned leaves can be found on *Hosta*, mint (*Mentha suaveolens* 'Variegata'), *Chlorophytum* and many other ornamental foliage plants (see White, p. 40).

● Silvery white seed clusters are produced by many wild *Clematis* and grasses (see Grasses, p. 44).

Leaves and berries create beautiful colour impressions in autumn.

Berries, fruits and leaves in all colours

Many shrubs do not make an impact until the autumn, when their foliage turns the most beautiful shades of yellow through dark red. Many trees and bushes display attractive berries, usually in shades of orange and red. The berries remain there well into winter and often represent the last splash of colour on your balcony. The soft, often silvery, shining tufts of some seed heads form an enchanting eye-catching feature. In winter, when decorated with snow, such heads resemble fluffy little balls. Multi-coloured foliage plants are decorative all year round.

Ornamental foliage plants with white variegation.

Ground cherry fruits (Physalis).

Red Pernettya berries.

Clematis seed heads.

A symphony of colour

The effects of sunlight on colours

You will find the optimal colour for your balcony or patio by observing the light conditions very carefully: each colour will have a different effect depending on the intensity of the light.

Delicate pastel shades look best in **soft light.**

Brilliant sunlight brings out the more saturated colours and makes them glow (see Opaqueness, p. 8).

Colours with less saturation, that is pastel shades, will quickly bleach in very bright sunlight.

You also need to think about what times of day you are most likely to use the balcony or patio:

In the mornings the sunlight has a large amount of blue in it. A blue flower will, therefore, seem fresh and intense in the morning. Leaf green looks particularly crisp in morning light (see Blue, p. 38; Green, p. 42).

In the afternoons the sunlight has a higher percentage of red and yellow. The glowing appearance of the blue flowers is lost from midday onwards, green looks a little drier. Yellow and red flowers, on the other hand, appear most brilliant and attractive in the afternoon (see Yellow and orange. p. 24; Red, p. 28).

The right position

The light conditions not only influence the appearance of colours but are also responsible for plant growth. Plants have differing requirements for light and temperature, too.

● South-facing balconies are very sunny, and will allow the unhindered penetration of sunlight. At the height of the summer season it may become very hot and dry here.

Suitable: In such a very sunny position, plants should be able to cope with dry periods. An ideal design would be a Mediterranean balcony with large container plants like oleander, *Bougainvillea*, passion flower and *Chrysanthemum*. If you water and fertilize sufficiently, balcony flowers like cranesbill and *Pelargonium* will also flourish here (see The correct way to water, p. 52).

● East- or west-facing positions are generally bright. Morning or afternoon sunlight ensures a balanced climate. Perennial woody plants on an east-facing balcony should be protected from cold, east winds (see Overwintering, p. 55).

Suitable: Nearly all balcony flowers flourish well here. For an unprotected, west-facing position, choose plants with rain-resistant flowers like *Scaevola*, bur marigold (*Bidens*) and verbena.

● Semi-shady or shady balconies generally face north, although a balcony or patio pointing east, south or west may be overshadowed by high trees. Overhanging roofs and other buildings will often plunge them into cool darkness. Here it is usually moister and cooler than in bright positions.

Suitable: Choose plants that will grow well even with little light and warmth. Try busy Lizzie (*Impatiens*), *Begonia* and *Fuchsia*, of which countless varieties cover the entire colour spectrum.

Boxes, containers and pots

Every plant on a balcony or patio requires a container in which its roots will find water and nourishment. Almost any container is suitable, provided excess water can drain away. Your choice of containers will also complement the colour design. Pots and boxes in many colours and styles are made in glazed pottery or plastics. White, red and brown terracotta and clay pots will lend a Mediterranean aura to your balcony.

My tip: Fibreglass containers are particularly suitable for colour design as you can paint them any shade you like.

This combination of strong and slightly saturated colours will cast a spell even on a narrow balcony.

Principles of design in practice

Your plant groupings are bound to succeed if you follow these design hints and tips.

Combining shapes
Illustration 1

For this design you should, if possible, combine plants of different heights and shapes of growth.

1 Growth habits: trailing, semi-erect, erect.

The size of a plant determines what function it will assume in the overall design:
● Tall plants make good accents as they can draw attention towards a certain direction especially if prominently coloured. In addition, tall plants can, if required, create a visual screen.
● Medium-sized plants can be subordinated to larger ones, in order to give them a firmer hold. If they are planted at a slight distance from taller plants, they will establish an extra, slightly more subdued highlight.
● Small plants form a connection between the accents not only by filling up gaps but also by supplying a basic colour.
The overall shape of a plant as well as its colour and height affect a design (see illustration 1):
● Plants with an erect habit are, for example,

heliotrope, *Zinnia* and many varieties of *Dianthus*. Climbing plants are also able to grow upwards by clinging to a climbing frame.
● Semi-erect plants will only stay erect in their lowest parts. The tips of their shoots will hang outwards, as with many types of busy Lizzie and many ornamental grasses.
● Trailing plants are, for example, *Lobelia*, bird's foot trefoil (*Lotus corniculatus*) and many *Petunia*. Arrange the plants in their container in such a way that the erect ones form a background for the planting. The semi-erect plants will appear in the middle foreground. At the front, where they are most visible, plant the trailers so they can curl around the edge of the container.
The size of the flowers and leaves:
Large, clear surfaces among flowers and leaves have a calming effect. Complicated shapes with small parts are enlivening (see photo, p. 13).

Delicate, small leaves can easily be used as a connecting theme.

Maintaining the balance
Illustrations 2 to 4

Designs are perceived as harmonious if they incorporate something that balances them – in the truest sense of the word. The habits, sizes and the colours should be balanced between the left and right sides. Really successful designs usually follow the classic, tried-and-tested principles of symmetry or asymmetry – whichever is appropriate. In each setting, you should decide on one of these principles in order to give your composition maximum effect.
Symmetrical designs should be used wherever a more geometrical or severe expression is needed.
● Similar plants are grouped in a mirror-image sequence either side of a central axis.
● The composition should incorporate a tall plant, as a central accent, that also

stands out for its colour. Whether you wish to accentuate the centre (see illustration 3) or prefer to establish accents at the sides (see illustration 4) will depend on your own taste and other considerations within the allotted space. Two centres of gravity on either side will help a group to hold together better. A central focus on the other hand will emphasize a smaller composition.

● Cool colours such as blue and white underline the geometrical character (see photo, p. 41).

● An outstanding, preferably complementary colour should be reserved for the tallest plant (see Contrasts, p. 11).

Asymmetrical designs appear livelier, are often filled with more tension and are multi-faceted (see illustration 2).

● The arrangement cannot be divided into two mirror-image halves as the main accent has been shifted to one side.

● The order of the plants should still be

2 An asymmetrical design with neighbouring colours, in which the main focus is to one side.

3 A symmetrical design with dark blue and red, in which the centre is emphasized.

4 A symmetrical design in which the corners are emphasized and the centre is highlighted with colour.

well balanced, and an alternative highlight should be formed opposite the most conspicuous plant by introducing a lower-growing, less accentuated plant.

● The distribution of the main and additional accents – together with lower-growing, other tall plants and groundcover – should be chosen in such a way that their impacts still balance once another.

● Accompanying plants should ideally combine accents so that their silhouette forms a non-equilateral triangle.

● Similar or the same plants should be placed at varying distances from the central motif. These create additional tension.

● Warm and cool colours are effective in asymmetrical designs. All tried-and-tested combinations can be used (see Colour harmonies, p. 10).

● Individual, contrasting colours lend greater weight to a highlight (see Contrasts, p. 11).

A flower palette

The following pages will provide you
with all the necessary know-how so that
you can successfully put together a
really splendid colour combination. We
will show you where and how to employ
each colour skilfully and which plants
are best for the purpose.

*Above: The colour orange glows among the dark
green foliage.*
*Left: The grey and silvery leaves of many herbs
and spicy plants create a harmonious picture
when combined with heavy terracotta
containers, the gravely path and the blue-tinged
flowers of lavender, periwinkle and blue
Spiraea.*

A flower palette

A riot of colour

Colourful windowboxes create a lively and happy atmosphere on your balcony. They have a friendly, often even playful affect, and if you use plants that have not been altered too much by the propagator, their colourful flowers will often conjure up a rustic, cottage-garden charm.

For a strong, colourful aura, plant flowers in the three primary colours (yellow, red and blue) between succulent green foliage. Individual splashes of the corresponding contrasting colour will make the total picture even livelier (see Understanding colours, p. 8). Pay attention to a balanced distribution of individual colours. Yellow has a great deal of brilliance and should therefore not be used too much: only about half as many yellow flowers are needed as red ones and only a quarter of the amount of blue flowers. Only in this way will red and blue not be overshadowed by the brilliance of yellow (see Yellow and orange, p. 24; Red, p. 28; Blue, p. 38).

A slightly more mellow impression can be achieved by strongly accentuating mixtures of colours (see Understanding colours, p. 8). White lightens all colourful pictures and makes the colours livelier (see White, p. 40). Tips for designs in which one colour dominates are given on pp. 24–45.

Flower colours

The following pages depict all that is important when combining plants and colours – whether yellows, pinks, greens or blues. They will describe the characteristics and special features of all colours in order to help you select the hues best suited to your balcony or patio.

The correct way to use a colour: This section will tell you whether a colour is better suited for large or small balconies and patios (see The effect of colours, p. 12). In addition it describes the kind of light and the optimum time of day that each colour will be most effective (see The effects of sunlight on colours, p. 16).

Effective combinations: Here we discuss the effect of every colour in the classic combinations: several shades of the same colour, colour runs, colour accords, contrasting colours and colourful arrangements (see Colour harmonies, p. 10).

Planting examples: Photographs of splendid plant arrangements in every colour will give you ideas, and precise descriptions will help you recreate them yourself. We will tell you the optimum position, the most important plant care needs and which containers and plants were used. Information on correct planting can be found on p. 50. More detailed information on general care is given on p. 52.

Further species: Plant lists incorporating every colour will make it easier to adapt the examples given. Even if you want to realize your very own ideas, you will find here a selection of the most beautiful species. Use of exact botanical names of the various varieties will prevent confusion (see Plant names, p. 56).

● The plant lists have been ordered according to each plant's growth habit. For a successful colour design it is very important to arrange the different shapes skilfully in a container (see Combining shapes, p. 18).

How to do it: Plant trailing plants at the front edge of the container, insert semi-erect species in the central area, and place erect or climbing plants at the back.

● The flowering time of each plant is given in brackets.

● The nutritional requirement of each plant is also provided (see Types of fertilizer, p. 53).

Important: Combine only those plants in a container that have the same feeding requirements so that you discourage pests and diseases caused by over- or underfertilizing (see Healthy balcony plants, p. 53).

Flower power in a flower tower: a cheerful mix of flowers occupies this floral display in which the primary colours (yellow, blue and red) are represented by plants of a wild flower character. Yellow and red dandelions and nasturtiums as well as morning glory have grown into the statice (Limonium), light blue Lobelia and black-eyed Susan, thus creating a tangle that is endlessly varied and fascinating.

Yellow and orange – Glowing sunny colours

A patio or balcony will have a tropical atmosphere when decorated with the colours of citrus fruits. Bright and cheerful like the sun, these colours will make you forget bad weather. Even with an overcast sky, they will help lift the mood by their cheerful nature.

Yellow is one of the three primary colours in the colour wheel (see Understanding colours, p. 8). Mixed with red it produces orange, and egg-yolk-coloured Indian yellow forms a transitional colour. Yellow and orange are known as warm colours – yellow forming the very core of the warm part of the spectrum. Orange too has a warming effect but does not attain the same degree of brilliance as yellow.

The correct way to use yellows and oranges

Yellow and orange are ideal to bridge large distances. They attract attention as they guide light rays into otherwise ignored parts. If you want to make spacious areas seem more cosy, try yellow and orange (see Designing spaces, p. 13). To enjoy their fullest intensity, use them on a balcony that you frequent in the evening (see The effects of sunlight on colours, p. 16).

Effective combinations

Shades of orange and yellow: A design incorporating light yellow flowers may appear light and frothy but also slightly reserved and elegant. The more orange the shade, the warmer and livelier the display will become.

Colour runs: Orange and green are neighbours of yellow. Combinations with light green in particular help yellow look very attractive (see photo, p. 26 right; Green, p. 42). A small quantity of red in a mainly orange design will underline the warm character.

Accords: Yellow flowers go well with red or blue, which they complement to form a trio (see Blue, p. 38; Red, p. 28). When these have been lightened to form light blue and pink, the yellow should also be more delicate (see Opaqueness, p. 8). A strong shade of orange goes better with its trio partners violet and green if these two are less saturated (see Green, p. 42; Violet, p. 36).

Contrasts in a sea of yellow flowers can be achieved with violet splashes. Blue-violet appears warmer with Indian yellow. Or decide on shades of orange with cool blue (see Violet, p. 36; Blue, p. 38). Always consider the enormous light-dark contrast of these colours. Even a few splashes of contrasting colour lend spatial depth and liveliness to a yellow design and will increase its brilliance further still.

My tip: Combine yellow with white and blue to make similarly lively but less harshly contrasting displays.

Colourful: Used sparingly, shades of yellow will bring panache without dominating the picture. Individual pale yellow flowers lend a special airiness to a design.

A yellow balcony
Photo p. 25

This summer design refreshes a sunny balcony. Plant *Cassia corymbosa*, patio rose, two *Rudbeckia hirta*, two *Melampodium paludosum* in terracotta containers. In the box, plant a *Sanvitalia procumbens* on each side, and in the centre a *Gazania*. All these plants are moderate feeders.

The full beauty of this yellow balcony unfolds in the warm afternoon light.

A flower palette

A yellow-and-red colour run with violet accents.

Light colours are excellent for a hanging basket.

Yellow and orange – Ideal colours for hanging baskets

A balcony or patio will always have only limited space for potted plants. Using vertical areas releases extra surfaces for containers without a great deal of effort: there will generally be more room for a hanging basket on a ceiling or wall. Light colours like yellow and orange are eminently suitable for a miniature hanging garden: the higher a plant is fixed, the lighter and more "lightweight" should be the colour you choose.

Yellow-and-red hanging basket
Photo top left

This hanging basket contains neighbouring colours from yellow to red with a complementary accent: the dark violet of the sweet-smelling heliotrope lends depth and tension to the design. *Lantana* gradually changes its colour so you should find many nuances from yellow to red on the same plant. The yellow *Helichrysum* will flower continuously all summer.
Container: A hanging basket with a diameter of 30 cm (12 in).

Position and care: Sun; moderate feeder.
Plants used: An erect *Heliotropium arborescens*; for semi-erect plants, one each of *Bracteantha bracteata* 'Dargan Hill Monarch' and *Lantana camara*.

Yellow à la crème
Photo top right

This hanging basket group is particularly light and frothy. The *Lantana* has yellow-variegated leaves and deep yellow, saturated flowers. We selected the cream-coloured *Helichrysum* for its velvety soft leaves. Its orange-coloured flowers *Helichrysum* smell of pineapple.
Container: A hanging basket with a diameter of 30 cm (12 in).
Position and care: Sun; moderate feeder.
Plants used: One each of semi-erect *Helichrysum thianschanicum* 'Goldkind', *Lantana* 'Aloha' and *Helichrysum petiolare* 'Roundabout'.

A spring idyll in a strawberry pot
Photo p. 27

"Pockets" on several levels make this container very practical and large enough for numerous plants without requiring much space itself. You can plant it year-round or alternate according to the season. In our example, the charming tulips look particularly attractive with a colour run from yellow to orange-red. A contrast is provided by the violet pansies.

Position and care: Shade to semi-shade; little fertilizer.

Plants used: 14 *Tulipa* 'Sundance' (Greigii); per pocket one *Viola cornuta* 'Princess Blue'.

Further species: Yellow

Erect habit: Gross feeders for a bright position are *Argyranthemum frutescens* 'Cornish Gold' (ES–MA), *Gazania* 'Mini Star Yellow' (LSP–EA); for full sun to semi-shade *Tagetes tenuifolia* 'Golden Gem' (LSP–MA). Moderate feeders are *Melampodium paludosum* 'Showstar' (LSP–EA), and for semi-shade to shade

Strawberry pots are good for saving space.

ornamental *Origanum vulgare* 'Aureum'.

Semi-erect: Moderate feeders are *Calceolaria integrifolia* 'Sunshine' (LSP–EA) for semi-shade, *Begonia* x *tuberhybrida* 'Trumpet Yellow', 'Nonstop Yellow' (LSP–MA) for shade.

Trailing: *Sanvitalia*

procumbens 'Irish Eyes' (LSP– MA) is a moderate feeder; *Bidens ferulifolia* 'Golden Eye' (LSP–MA) is a gross feeder and needs sun. *Dyssodia tenuiloba* (LS–EA) requires little fertilizer and a bright position.

Further species: Orange

Erect habit: Moderate feeders are *Tagetes tenuifolia* 'Tangerine Gem' and 'Safari Tangerine' (LSP–MA) and *Rudbeckia hirta* 'Toto' (MS–MA) for full sun to semi-shade. *Begonia* x *tuberhybrida* 'Nonstop Orange' (LSP–MA) and *Fuchsia* 'Göttingen' (LSP–MA) like a bright to shady position; *Zinnia haageana* 'Classic' (MS–MA) needs sun to semi-shade.

Semi-erect: *Impatiens walleriana* 'Accent Orange Star' (LSP–MA) likes it to be sunny to shady with moderate amounts of fertilizer in semi-shade to shade.

Trailing: *Begonia pendula* 'Illumination Orange' (LSP–MA) requires moderate amounts of fertilizer in semi-shade to shade.

Climbing: *Thunbergia* loves full or moderate sun. *T.* 'Ladylike' (ES–MA) is a gross feeder and *T. alata* (LSP–MA) a moderate one. Runner beans are gross feeders for bright positions.

Red – A fiery temperament

The colour red impresses with its passion. Laden with energy and very stimulating, it is just the colour for recharging the batteries. In order to avoid it becoming too dominant, it should be used only with great care in larger quantities.

Red is a primary colour like yellow and blue (see Understanding colours, p. 8). Among the shades of red are also counted yellow mixtures like orange-red – also purple and lilac, both of which have some parts of blue. The spectrum reaches from very warm shades right into the cool, blue range.

The correct way to use reds

Red attains its greatest intensity in the warm, evening light (see The effects of sunlight on colours, p. 16), although, in the morning, light red flowers with their great brilliance will not be overlooked. They will attract attention over over great distances,

so that just a few splashes of strong red as accents are eye-catching (see Designing spaces, p. 13). A single plant like *Canna indica* will conjure up warmth and cheer in otherwise unattractive corners. The great effectiveness at a distance of red flowers provides an increased sense of unity to an uninviting patio. Accordingly you should plant only sparingly in confined spaces.

Effective combinations

Light red flowers will only allow other colours, especially darker ones, to dominate if the other flowers are in greater

quantity.

Dark red flowers, on the other hand, seem to blend into darker coloured surroundings, and a rather melancholy total impression can then result. To make dark red stand out against its background, surround it with lighter shades like white (see p. 40), yellow (see p. 24) or pink (see p. 32).

Combining shades of red is rarely possible with plants: almost always contrasting green foliage will prevent a monochrome impression from being achieved. You can try to "push back" the green by introducing red pots and accessories, or else you could use extensive silvery foliage, but this will also tend to subdue a little the gushing temperament of the total impression. (see photo, p. 30).

Colour runs: Not all shades of red can readily be grouped together. As red is situated at the changeover from the warm to the cool part of the spectrum, shrill combinations can

quickly arise (see Understanding colours, p. 8). White or strong green can be used as a mediator (see White, p. 40; Green, p. 42). To avoid any risks, select colours in only one direction away from red: via lilac to violet and blue; or via orange to yellow (see Blue, p. 38; Yellow and orange, p. 24).

Accords: Shades of blue have a calming, cooling effect on fiery red. When further complemented by yellow, you have the trio of primary colours.

Contrasts with red will always be present in any plant design through the constant presence of foliage that is almost always green. Should you wish to heighten the effect, choose if possible light red flowers and very dark green foliage (see Green, p. 42).

Colourful: A colourful arrangement can be invigorated by a few single red flowers. If present in too large quantities, red flowers will quickly dominate and turn other colours into background scenery.

The red cactus Dahlia in the foreground form wonderful flower balls that contrast well with the long, erect racemes of Lobelia x speciosa 'Compliment Scarlet'. Both need moderate amounts of fertilizer as do the plants in the red painted box: Salvia coccinea 'Lady in Red', Mentha suaveolens 'Variegata' and Lotus berthelotii. The grey, needle-like, small leaves of the Lotus soften the boundaries and dampen down the contrast between the red flowers and the green leaves – just as the cool violet colour does in the gross feeder Solanum rantonnetii in the container on the left. All these plants require full sun.

A flower palette

Small but delicate
Photo right

This small box combines dark red flowers with brilliant silvery foliage in such a way that the whole ensemble assumes an elegant, totally satisfying look (see White, p. 40).
Container: A box 60 cm (24 in) long, 10 cm (4 in) wide.
Position and care: Bright sun to semi-shade; gross feeders.
Plants used: Two red, ivy-leaved, trailing *Pelargonium* e.g. 'Tavira'; one each of semi-erect *Helichrysum petiolare* and *H.p.* 'Roundabout'.

Further species: Cool red

Erect habit: Zonal *Pelargonium* 'Brasil' and 'Garnet' (LSP–MA) are gross feeders in semi-shade to full sun. Medium feeders are *Dianthus chinensis* 'Fire Carpet' (LSP–EA) in sun to semi-shade and *Gomphrena globosa* 'Buddy' (ES–MA) for fully sunny to bright positions.

An elegant but still lively composition with geraniums and Helichrysum.

Semi-erect: Fuchsia 'Winston Churchill' (LSP–MA) will thrive in in a shady to semi-shady position with moderate amounts of fertilizer.
Trailing: Pelargonium peltatum 'Maya' and 'Comedy' (LSP–MA) are gross feeders of fertilizer for semi-shady to very bright positions, as are *Petunia surfinia* 'Shihi Brilliant' (LSP–MA), *P.* 'Million Bells' (LSP–MA) and *Verbena tenera* 'Cleopatra' (ES–MA).

Further species: Warm red

Erect habit: Zonal *Pelargonium* 'Highfield's Pride' and *P.* 'Deacon Summertime' (LSP–MA) are gross feeders and *Tagetes tenuifolia* 'Red Gem' (LSP–MA) and *Dahlia* 'Feuerrad' (ES–LA) are moderate feeders; all like semi-shade to full sun. Moderate feeding is required by *Begonia* x *tuberhybrida* 'Switzerland' (LSP–MA) *and Fuchsia* 'Kwintett' (LSP–MA) in semi-

shade to shade, by *Celosia argentea cristata* 'Jewel Box Mixed' in bright to full sun, and by *Nicotiana* x *sanderae* 'Nicki Red' (ES–MA) in bright to semi-shady positions.
Semi-erect: Moderate feeders in bright to semi-shady spots are *Impatiens walleriana* 'Accent Red' (LSP–MA) and *Phlox drummondii* 'Dwarf Scarlet' (ES–MA).
Trailing: Gross feeders in full sun are *Pelargonium peltatum* 'Fire Cascade' (LSP–MA) and *Petunia solana*

'Fergy' (LSP–MA) as well as *Petunia* 'Hit Parade Rot' (LSP–MA). A moderate feeder in semi-shade to shade is *Fuchsia* 'Arcadia' (LSP–MA).
Climbing:
Eccremocarpus scaber (ES–MA) is a moderate feeder in bright positions.

A red design with good taste
Photo top right

Decorative fruit and vegetables can make an elegant colour design out of a tasteful one. Runner beans and gourds that quickly cover an entire wall on an espalier also provide an attractive form of visual screen (see Climbing aids, p. 54). Trees and bushes require sufficient room for their usually spreading growth as well as generous-sized pots, in which they can thrive for a few years. They prefer a few hours of full sun, particularly during the ripening period.
Container: A large container with a

These colourful berries are both delicious and fun.

Succulent red currants.

Attractive ruby chard.

diameter of 40 cm (16 in), strawberry pot (see p. 27).
Position and care: Semi-shade to full sun; moderate feeders, except strawberries which need little fertilizer.
Plants used: In a large container, currants 'Red Lake' and 'Rondom' with wild strawberries as an underplanting. Strawberry 'Elsanta' in a strawberry pot.

Further varieties of fruit and vegetables

Red: Runner bean, tomatoes 'Totem', 'Tumbler', 'Red Robin', 'Brasero', a pepper plant, raspberries, apple tree 'Ballerina' varieties 'Waltz', 'Polka' and 'Bolero'.
Yellow: Gooseberry 'Invicta', raspberry 'All Gold'.
Blue: Blueberries, runner bean 'Purple Teepee'.
Dark violet: Aubergine 'Mini Bambino'.
Green: Curly lettuce 'Salad Bowl', fine curly lettuce 'Frisby' as well as light green cropping lettuce 'Tom Thumb'.

Pink – A colour with many faces

Delicate romanticism, discreet charm, the shocking pink of youth or relaxed elegance – pink allows you to paint a wide range of very different pictures. It has always been very popular for all designs with balcony flowers, and there are countless species and cultivars in pink.

Some very different shades of colour all fall under the heading of "pink": from light violet through to light cinnabar-red. It seems hard, however, to fit "shocking pink" with its brilliance and such a subdued colour as "lilac" – both with large proportions of blue – in this pink category (see Understanding colours, p. 8). Partially opaque purple is often referred to as "rose" and light cinnabar-red, with its higher proportion of yellow, is sometimes termed "old rose".
In keeping with this wide range of pinks, different shades can be perceived as cool or warm, depending on their proportions of blue or yellow (see Colour connections, p. 9).

The correct way to use pinks

Pink flowers often create a loud effect or a visual firework display on a balcony or patio. The more delicate nuances with less saturation, like lilac, salmon or old rose, will unfold their charm nearer to the observer (see Understanding colours, p. 8). They are, therefore, particularly suited to small, narrow positions that may attract more notice through the use of these pale shades (see Designing spaces, p. 13).
Pink may be so pale that it seems to shine out from shady corners like precious stones. Even in the light of dawn or dusk, it still glows visibly. In very bright light, however, it can look pale and colourless (see The effects of sunlight on colours, p.16).

Effective combinations

Choose partners for pink flowers from the same range of the spectrum to be certain of a successful design. Combine a bluish pink with colours from the cool range, and a yellowish pink with colours from the warm part of the spectrum (see Colour connections, p. 9).
Shades of pink: Compositions that include various saturated pinks tend to radiate a particular charm and liveliness

Callistephus chinensis.

(see Opaqueness, p. 8 and photo, p. 33)
You also need to consider the "temperature" of the colours: combine only cool or only warm shades of pink with each other (see Colour harmonies. p. 10).
Colour runs: Pink combined with light blue is very romantic. With darker blue, the elegant character of the pink flowers would be emphasized (see Blue, p. 38).
Accords: Choose a complementary colour from the pastel shades of pink in order to maintain a balance: pink with light blue or palest yellow appears light and cheerful (see Yellow, p. 24; Blue, p. 38).
Contrasts are achieved with colours from green through to yellow – depending on the strength of the pink. Green forms a contrast to light red (see Green, p. 42). The darker the green in which you embed the pink flowers, the stronger will be the contrast of light and dark in addition to the contrast between the

complementary colours: the pale flowers will appear even lighter, the dark foliage even heavier. The contrast will, conversely, be weakened if you select pale foliage, for example leaves with a silvery grey sheen (see White, p. 40). The pink will be emphasized and the design will be very lively.

More bluish pinks will go very well with silvery grey foliage, although the complementary colour is yellow (see Yellow, p. 24). Very strong yellow together with a delicate pink may, however, appear very "loud". This is why we recommend choosing a shade of yellow that is just as delicate as the pink, and even this yellow should be employed very sparingly.

Colourful: In a mixture of strong colours, pink can succeed only if it appears in large quantities. In a group of very colourful pastel shades, pink will provide a balancing and subtly flattering element.

A romantic balcony with profuse rose and mallow flowers.

A romantic balcony
Photo above

The pale pink flowers on the standard rose and the slightly darker, wafer-thin petals of the mallow are very harmonious together. In the summer, the delicate shades and shapes will provide a dream-like picture. In the autumn, the colour of the pink roses will deepen slightly.

Containers: Three large containers with a diameter of 40 cm (16 in), one container with a diameter of 30 cm (12 in).

Position and care: Full sun; moderate feeders.

Plants used: In the larger container, a standard rose (*Rosa moschata* 'Ballerina') and a mallow (*Lavatera olbia* 'Barnsley'). In the smaller container, an erect, floribunda-type bedding rose (*R.* 'Bonica') underplanted with a ground-covering, polyantha-type rose (*R.* 'The Fairy').

My tip: The roses will continue flowering right until the first frosts if you always prune back each shoot below the first "eye" immediately after it has flowered.

A flower palette

Pink in autumn
Photo right

This pink/red autumnal design will still look good well into winter – the flowers being almost preserved by frost.
Containers: Two boxes 80 cm (32 in) long, 20 cm (8 in) wide. Two pots each with a diameter of 15 cm (6 in).
Position and care: Very bright to shady. No fertilizer needed.
Plants used: In one box: at the back, three *Erica gracilis*; at the front, a *Chrysanthemum indicum* and a *Hedera helix*. In the second box: at the back, four *Erica*; at the front, two *Chrysanthemum*. In the pots *Pernettya mucronata* and *Carex morrowii*.

A red and pink autumn duo of Erica and Chrysanthemum with some greenery.

Pink, blue and white in spring ...
Photo p. 35 top

The strong pinks of many spring-flowering plants like *Bellis perennis* and *Dicentra spectabilis* are particularly refreshing after a grey winter. White and orange, miniature *Narcissus* 'Geranium', blue *Muscari armeniacum* and light blue *Myosotis sylvatica* will enrich the picture (see White, p. 40; Blue, p. 38). Pink also looks good with young foliage on *Carex morrowii* and *Hosta* 'White Brim' (see Green, p. 42).

... and in the summer

In summer, exchange the faded bulbous flowers and *Bellis* for the pink and blue arrangement (see photo, p. 35).
Recommended plants: Together with bleeding heart, plant a

Delicate Convolvulus.

busy Lizzie (*Impatiens walleriana* 'Pink Swirl'); in the bowl on the right three *Lobelia erinus* 'Azuro'; in the top bowl *Diascia vigilis* 'Jack Elliott' (see photos, p. 37).

Further species: Cool pink

Erect habit: moderate feeders in semi-shade to full sun are *Verbena* 'Armour Light Pink' (ES–MA), *Antirrhinum majus* 'Lipstick Silver' (LSP–MA); in semi-shade to shade *Fuchsia* 'Cliantha' (LSP–MA). Moderate feeder *Gypsophila repens* 'Rosea' (ES–EA) likes sun to semi-shade.

Semi-erect: A moderate feeder in full sun to semi-shade is *Alyssum maritimum* 'Oriental Night' (LSP–MA). *Phlox drummondii* 'Double Chanel' (MS–EA) prefers sun to semi-shade, and *Impatiens* New Guinea 'Tango' (LSP–MA) likes semi-shade to shade.

Trailing: Moderate feeders are *Centradenia* 'Cascade' (ES–MA) in sun to full sun, *Lobelia erinus compacta* 'Rosamund' (LSP–MA) in sun to semi-shade. Zonal *Pelargonium* 'Blues' (LSP–EA) is a gross feeder in full sun.

Climbing: Moderate feeders in sun are *Lathyrus latifolius* 'Rosa Perle' and *Asarina barclayana* (ES–EA).

Cool pink with neighbouring blue and white flowers in spring.

Further species: Warm pink

Erect habit: *Begonia* x *tuberhybrida* 'Nonstop Pink' (LSP–MA) is a moderate feeder in

Eye-catching Dianthus.

semi-shade to shade. Zonal *Pelargonium* 'Clorinda' (LSP–MA) is a gross feeder in semi-shade to full sun.

Semi-erect: Moderate feeders *Impatiens walleriana* 'Super Elfin Lipstick' and dwarf *Impatiens* 'Victorian Rose' (LSP–MA) thrive in shade or sun.

Trailing: *Pelargonium* 'Ville de Paris' (LSP–MA) is a gross feeder in a semi-shady to full sunny position.

Climbing: *Rhodochiton atrosanguineus* (LSP–MA) is a moderate feeder in sun, and *Asarina erubescens* (MS–MA) is a gross feeder in full sun.

A violet pansy.

Violet – The colour of *Viola*

A mixture of red and blue produces violet – a truly charming colour for flowers. Very often the basic dark violet colour can also be found in lighter variations (see Opaqueness, p. 8). Combinations of flowers with varying amounts of opaqueness and saturation are particularly interesting: from the deepest shade of violet via strong pink to cheerful rose-pink (see Understanding colours, p. 8; Pink, p. 32). Some flowers include all this attractive colour range in each individual petal.

Spectacular flowerers: Petunia Surfinia 'Pastel' and 'Million Bells'.

Adjacent colours of different intensities.

Nature uses the contrasting effect of complementary colours very successfully. To attract bees, the violet pansy has a yellow eye while the abundant flowers of Petunia 'Million Bells' lure bees with glowing yellow centres, surrounded by brilliant lilac.

Diascia vigilis and Osteospermum.

Petunia 'Blue Vein'.

Petunia 'Blue', geranium 'Casanova'.

Blue – The colour of infinite spaces

The colour blue creates a peaceful, pleasant, cool atmosphere. Some light blue flowers have the same effect as a brilliant spring sky, while dark blue flowers seem as though they have just arisen from the depths of the sea.

Blue is particularly suitable for small balconies.

Blue, red and yellow form the three primary colours (Understanding colours, p. 8). Pure blue can appear as midnight-blue or by being lightened can turn into pale blue. Blue mixed with red forms violet, while yellow shifts the colour towards blue-green. Blue is the coolest hue in the colour wheel and, after violet, also the darkest.

The correct way to use blues

Blue requires a great deal of light to be fully effective, and is strongest in bright morning light. It will not stand out in shade nor over great distances (see The effects of sunlight on colours, p. 16). In poor light, a blue design will quickly look melancholy or heavy. When placed a little behind other colours, blue gives an impression of spatial depth even in fairly shallow displays. This is why blue flowers are well suited to visually enlarging small balconies (see Designing spaces, p. 13; and photo right). At the same time, blue makes a sunny spot appear refreshing, cooling, peaceful and relaxing. With the right furnishings and good design, blue can look distant and elegant (see Principles of design in practice, p. 18).

Effective combinations

A saturated blue looks distinguished when alternated with white flowers. Even small arrangements will appear larger (see White, p. 40).
Shades of blue with exclusively dark tints may look heavy. Add light blue to lighten the effect.
Colour runs of blue can be formed with blue and red mixtures like violet and purple, or with green (see Green, p. 42). These colours all harmonize well. A little white or a pale neighbouring colour will open up groups of flowers with fully saturated colours (see Opaqueness, p. 8; White, p. 40).

For a colour accord, complement blue with red and yellow (see Yellow, p. 24; Red, p. 28). To combine blue with only red, select a pale shade so the arrangement does not look too heavy.
Contrasts: Used sparingly, warm orange strengthens the cool aura of blue. Blue flowers will have a pleasantly calming effect in colourful arrangements (see A riot of colour, p. 22).

These colours and scents evoke memories of southern France.

Blue creates space
Photo left

This sunny balcony with summer flowers in blue and neighbouring pink does not look cramped although the area is small. In a container (60 x 30 cm/ 24 x 12 in) several moderate feeders have been placed together: four *Campanula pyramidalis* at the sides, a *Felicia amelloides*, and four *Bacopa* as groundcover. In a box (100 x 20 cm/40 x 8 in) are several plants that need very little fertilizer: 12 *Viola* x *wittrockiana* Universal Plus 'True Blue' and three 'White Hotch'.

Blue with neighbouring plants
Photo above

A summery box filled with blue and violet-coloured flowers.
Container: A box 60 cm (24 in) wide, 15 cm (6 in) deep.
Position and care: Sun; moderate feeders.
Plants used: One each of erect *Heliotropium arborescens*, *Salvia farinacea* 'Victoria', trailing *Petunia* 'Frenzy Light Blue'; two semi-erect *Silene coeli-rosa* 'Blue Angel'.

Further species: Blue

Erect habit: *Viola* 'Joker Light Blue' (MSP–LS) are moderate feeders in sun to semi-shade, *Myosotis* 'Indigo' (ESP–LSP) in full sun to shade.

Semi-erect: Moderate feeders in full sun to semi-shade are *Lobelia erinus* 'Cambridge Blue' (LSP–MA) and *Phlox drummondii* 'Bobby Sox' (MS–EA).
Trailing: Gross feeders in full sun to semi-shade are *Petunia surfinia* 'Blue Vein' (LSP–MA) and *Scaevola aemula* 'Blue Wonder' (LSP–MA).
Climbing: Moderate feeders are *Ipomoea tricolor* 'Heavenly Blue' (MS–EA) in full sun to semi-shade, *Cobaea scandens* (MS–MA) in sun to semi-shade.

White – Expressive neutrality

In the heat of summer, white has a pleasant, refreshing effect as if it had saved something of the coolness of winter and carried it over into the warm part of the year. Brilliant white flowers and silvery grey foliage conjure up a calm atmosphere of elegance and pristine purity.

All colours on the colour wheel appear lighter when they are only slightly saturated (see Opaqueness, p. 8). Very pale yellows, for example, are described as yellowish white. If no colour is present, we have pure white. This pure white cannot be assigned to the cool or warm part of the spectrum (see Understanding colours, p. 8). It reacts completely neutrally in combinations. Even the slightest hint of any other colour will assign white to that part of the spectrum.

The correct way to use whites

Just like the colour blue, white also creates a feeling of distance and space. It can, therefore, make a small balcony appear larger (see The effect of colours, p. 12). White flowers hardly change their appearance during the daytime or evening as they reflect even very weak rays of light. This means they shine out in twilight and are able to attract attention in even the darkest corners (see The effects of sunlight on colours, p. 16).

Effective combinations

As soon as white assumes even a hint of another colour, you should refer to that new colour for design tips. Pure white can be combined with any colour. It can also be used between colours where direct contact is perceived as inharmonious. Even cool and warm shades of pink combine well in this way (see Pink, p. 32).

Important: White can quickly dominate and crowd out other leader colours if too much of it is used.

Using several **shades of white** can transform a design, especially with plants that have fairly severe shapes, which will become elegant and dignified. Playful shapes of flowers and a variety of silvery or white-variegated leaves on ornamental shrubs will, on the other hand, have a lively effect. **Delicate pink** will underline the peaceful aura of a white patio (see Pink, p. 32).

Yellow is a suitable partner for white as it is similarly brilliant (see Yellow, p 24) and they are ideal for shade and evening light (see The effects of sunlight on colours, p. 16).

White forms a *contrast* to all dark things. The contrast is greatest with black. As there are only very few plants that are close to black, you should use dark blue or dark red. These will lend even greater radiance to a mainly white design (see Red, p. 28; Blue, p. 38).

Colourful designs can be livened up by the use of white, which makes every other colour glow. White also provides an oasis of tranquillity amid a torrent of colours.

A truly dramatic colour for a small balcony.

Bundles of stars
Photo left

This cascade of flowers will bring an air of abundance to even a small balcony.
Container: A box 60 cm (24 in) long, 15 cm (6 in) wide.
Position and care: Full sun to semi-shade; gross feeder.
Plants used: At either side, an *Argyranthemum frutescens* 'Vera'; in the centre *Osteospermum* 'Whirlygig'.

A symmetrical composition in white.

Symmetry in white
Photo right

These container plants have been arranged strictly symmetrically on this autumnal balcony. Boxes of profusely flowering *Chrysanthemum* with white-variegated ivy form the centre of the composition.
The other containers are planted with *Chrysanthemum*, *Erica gracilis*, ivy, *Pernettya* and cone-shaped yews. The plants require a bright to shady position and no fertilizer.

Further species: White

Erect habit: The gross feeding zonal *Pelargonium* 'Carol Gibbons' (LSP–MA) is suitable for full sun to semi-shade, as is moderate feeding *Nicotiana* x *sanderae* 'Domino White' (ES–EA). Other moderate feeders: *Begonia* x *tuberhybrida* 'Nonstop White' (LSP–MA) in a bright to semi-shady position, and *Fuchsia* 'Annabel' (LSP–MA) in semi-shade to shade.

Semi-erect: A moderate feeder in sun or semi-shade is *Lobelia erinus compacta* 'White Fountain' (LSP–MA). *Impatiens walleriana* 'Accent White' (MS–MA) likes sun to semi-shade. Scented *Pelargonium* 'Lady Plymouth' is an ornamental foliage plant for a bright position.

Trailing: Gross feeders *Pelargonium peltatum* 'Luna' (LSP–MA) and *Petunia surfinia* 'White' (LSP–MA), and moderate feeder *Lobularia maritima* 'Snow Crystals' (LSP–MA) are all suited to full sun to semi-shade. *Sutera* 'Snowflake' (LSP–MA) is an ornamental foliage plant that requires moderate amounts of fertilizer in a bright position.

Climbing: *Solanum jasminoides* (ES–MA) needs large amounts of fertilizer as well as a position in full sun.

Green – Pure nature

The sight of succulent green foliage has a calming, soothing effect on humans. We connect the colour green with natural things as it is the dominant colour in nature. The green-colouring substance chlorophyll serves the most basic metabolic process in plants: together with sunlight it helps build up vital glucose, which is a plant's energy source.

An eye-catching, tiered display of container plants.

As with the colour red, the variations on green reach from the warm to the cool part of the spectrum. When it contains a large proportion of blue, it turns cool blue-green; when it has a large proportion of yellow, it appears lighter and warmer (see Understanding colours, p. 8).

The correct way to use greens

Green is contained as a basic framework in every group of plants; often it is the dominant colour. Green plants are ideal if your patio or balcony is a resting place after a day full of exertion or if you have little time or interest in more detailed care of flowering plants. Evergreens, in particular, make lovely ornamental plants all year round.

Effective combinations

Several *shades of green* create the only severely monochrome design that is possible and problem-free with plants. So that it is relaxing yet not entirely without tension, your design should emphasize the different growth habits (see illustration 1, p. 18; Structures, p. 44). *Colour runs* of yellow to blue-green, through pure green, should be combined with strong dark green, as yellow-green is assigned to the warm part of the spectrum and blue-green to the cool part (see Colour harmonies, p. 10). Colour runs from green to yellow (see Yellow, p. 24) or from green to blue (see Blue, p. 38) are simpler. For a *colour accord,* complement green with violet (Violet, see p. 36) and orange (see Yellow and orange, p. 24). Here too green will not just look like a "filler" if it can impress with its quantity and a special shape. *Contrasts* to a green design can be created with red flowers (see Red, p. 28). Choose green plants with a very defined shape so you

have something to set against the red brilliance. Or select a subdued wine-red in order to remove some of the severity from the composition.
Colourful designs can be rounded off with green, which is restful to the eye.

A herb garden
Photo left

A constant supply of fresh herbs for the preparation of delicious meals is very practical. Herbs with their variously shaped, often filigree foliage in all shades of green can also be very decorative. Sage 'Icterina', dill, rosemary, marjoram and thyme are growing on these herb steps.
My tip: Aromatic herbs like peppermint should be placed next to the sitting corner.
Further suitable herbs: Moderate feeding and lots of sun encourage the fragrance in basil, chamomile, lavender, lovage, tarragon and lemon balm. Borage, chervil, parsley and salad burnet prefer semi-

Lush green plants make this balcony a cosy place in which to relax.

shade. Marjoram and wormwood need little fertilizer.

Several shades of green
Photo above

A grapevine (*Vitis vinifera*) and other climbers as well as ornamental foliage transform this sunny balcony into a cosy bower (see Climbing aids, p. 54). A pineapple lily (*Eucomis comosa*) grows in a container with a diameter of 30 cm (12 in). In a box (100 x 20 cm/40 x 8 in) are moderate feeders *Euphorbia*, *Acorus gramineus*, *Bergenia cordifolia* 'Baby Doll', *Hedera helix* and *Hosta* 'White Brim'. *Pharbitis acuminata* grows in a hydroculture pot with a diameter of 60 cm (24 in) (see Hydroculture, p. 51).

Further species: Green

Erect habit: *Reseda odorata* is a small feeder in sun to semi-shade; *Plectranthus ciliatus* is a gross feeder in sun to shade, and *Moluccella laevis* and *Pelargonium* 'The Czar' are moderate feeders in full sun to semi-shade.
Semi-erect: Scented *Pelargonium capitatum* and *P. fragrans* are moderate feeders in full sun.
Trailing: Moderate feeders in sun to shade are *Ampelopsis brevipedunculata* and *Glechoma hederacea* 'Variegata', and in semi-shade is *Fragaria vesca*.

43

A flower palette

Structures
Photo right

When designing with flower colours, the shapes of leaves and flowers often tend to disappear in the background. When composing with beautiful foliage, the leaf structures become the main theme with many variations. You will find leaves that are smooth, wavy, hairy, curvy, toothed or deeply indented. There is also a wide range of size from small, needle-shaped leaves on ornamental asparagus through to the plate-sized leaves of *Hosta*. Grasses, in particular, charm with their interesting structure. Their gentle rustling has a calming effect on one's mood. Ornamental perennial grasses that remain small like *Carex* open up a severe-looking group of green conifers. Positioned individually, they are eye-catching; and when placed with colourful summer flowers, they make the whole picture more natural. The main

season for ornamental grasses is autumn, when their stalks turn yellowish, reddish or brownish. They will last until winter if sheltered from wind.

My tip: Do not cut off the stalks as they are attractive even in winter when they attract hoarfrost in bizarre shapes.

Container: A box 50 cm (20 in) long, 20 cm (8 in) wide.

Position and care: Sun to semi-shade; small feeder.

Plants used: One each of *Pennisetum compressum*, ice plant (*Sedum spectabile*), wood spurge (*Euphorbia amygdaloides* 'Purpurea') and heather (*Calluna vulgaris*).

Green wall
Photo, p. 45 top

Bamboo and grasses can form a green screen. *Fargesia murieliae* 'Simba' and *Panicum virgatum* are suitable for a balcony. Plant in containers with a diameter of 50 cm (20 in) and position in semi-shade.

Grasses such as these have enchanting forms.

Further species: Grasses

Plain green: For full sun try the small feeders *Lagurus ovatus, Achnatherum calamagrostis, Briza minor* and *B. maxima* as well as medium feeder *Pennisetum orientale*. Small feeders *Festuca gigantea* and *F. scoparia* require semi-shade.

Striped leaves: Try small feeders *Phalaris arundinacea* 'Tricolor' and *Spartina pectinata* 'Aureomarginata' in full sun as well as *Carex hachijoensis* in semi-shade.

Water plants on a balcony
Photo below

Water plants look very exclusive yet need little care. Even if there is little space, you need not forgo this kind of ornament.

Any watertight container can be utilized for a miniature water garden. Many water plants are suitable for very small containers: some will even cope with a water level of 10 cm (4 in). A miniature pond can be planted in spring or summer, suitable plants usually being sold in wire baskets. You should also be able to buy pond compost from specialist nurseries. For water lilies, mix flower compost with clay. This layer should be at least 10 cm (4 in) thick for larger water lilies.

How to plant in your water garden: Set the planted wire basket in the container and fill it up with compost. Then water the container thoroughly.

This grassy-screened balcony recreates the appearance of a river bank.

Suitable water and marginal plants

Moderate feeders like yellow *Caltha palustris*

Nymphaea tetragona 'Alba' for shallow pots.

(MSP–LSP), yellow *Iris pseudacorus* (LSP–MS) and small feeders like green *Juncus effusus* and yellow *Nymphoides peltata*

(MS–MS) all need full sun to semi-shade. *Typha minima* (ES–MS) with its blackish brown spadices (bulrushes) requires full sun and very little fertilizer. To form their flowers, water lilies need moderate feeding and at least six hours of sunshine per day: for water 10–20 cm (4–8 in) deep, *Nymphaea* 'Froebelii' (dark red), *N.* 'Maurice Laydeker' (purple red) and *N. tetragona* 'Helvola' (cream) will all be suitable.

Care &
maintenance

Healthy, thriving plants form the
foundation stone for a successful colour
design. The following pages show you
what to do so you can enjoy vigorous
plants with splendid flowers for the
entire season. Helpful tips will advise
you on planning, purchasing and
positioning of your balcony decor.

*Above: Celastrus orbiculatus branches are thickly
set with berries.*
*Left: In autumn, warm reds and yellows
dominate the scene. Profusely flowering
Chrysanthemum harmonizes beautifully with
decorative gourds, while the red berries on the
potted dwarf Cotoneaster will enrich the diet of
many birds.*

Care & maintenance

Using a plan when designing

Colour designing with balcony plants will be a success if you plan properly: work out the arrangement of plants and colours with a simple sketch. Use the same scale to depict all containers on the plan. Coloured crayons should indicate where and when which plants are to supply which colours for the total design. The sketch will serve as a shopping list that can be reused the following year or can be varied.

Important: At the planning stage, give some thought to the fact that only plants with the same moisture and nutrient requirements can be combined in the same container (see p. 52).

Buying plants

For healthy balcony plants we recommend delaying planting out until after the last frosts in spring. Although you can buy your plants before this, do not be tempted to start potting out early, because plants that have been spoiled by hothouse conditions may succumb to a late frost.

Signs to watch out for:
● Vigorous, green, new buds which promise abundant flowers.

● Plants that display compact growth.
● Plants that already display a few flowers so that you can be sure of having the right colour.
● Lots of white, many-branched roots. Lift the rootstock out of the pot to check.
● Unhealthy stock. Buy only plants without pests or diseases. Check all the leaves including their undersides.

My tip: The work of repotting and clearing rubbish away can be avoided if you choose plants that have been grown in decomposable pots. The pots can be planted in the potting compost, where they will quickly biodegrade.

Buying potting compost

Potting compost will give plant roots a firm hold as well as store water and nutrients. *Flowering plants* make heavy demand on nutrients (see Plants' nutritional needs, p. 53), and only a limited amount of compost can be accommodated in a balcony box. It is therefore important to fill the plant containers with fresh potting compost every year. Only in this way can you be sure of a basic supply of nutrients and a suitable medium in which to store water throughout the entire flowering season.

Hardy woody plants need fresh compost only every 2–3 years (see The correct way to plant, p. 50). To delay changing the compost for further two years, add about 40% broken-up Hortag to the compost. This will improve its environment so the plant can absorb the nutrients present in sufficient quantities. Plants that develop yellow leaves and no longer grow properly are generally lacking nutrients.

What you should look out for:
● If possible, choose a compost rich in clay, which ensures that the nutrient supply is released only on demand. Thus the plant is protected from overfeeding.
● Some potting composts are already enriched with fertilizer. The initial dose will last for the first six weeks. You will only need to add fertilizer if the plants are gross feeders (see Types of fertilizer, p. 53).
● For plants that require large quantities of fertilizer, buy a controlled-release fertilizer and mix it thoroughly into the potting compost (see Types of fertilizer, p. 53).
● Flowers in a hydroculture are planted in a type of compost called Hortag. This can be reused every year (see Hydroculture, p. 51). This will save you money and energy for purchasing and transporting compost.

This flower meadow in miniature in a colour trio is accompanied by white plants.

The correct way to plant

Some garden centres have facilities for planting purchased plants straight into boxes and other containers on their premises. This makes planning easier and saves much clearing and cleaning up at home. If you plant your plants at home, protect the floor with thick plastic sheeting or newspaper.

Preparing the containers
Illustration 1

Collect the boxes and containers together.

1 Inserting bubble wrap, and watering.

● Thoroughly clean out soil/compost remains from any container that has been used before, using hot liquid soap and a brush. This is to eradicate any disease-producing organisms.
● Punch or drill drainage holes in the bottom of any new container so that surplus water can drain away easily once the container is planted up.
● Improve the microclimate if necessary. Terracotta pots containing hardy woody plants should be lined inside with bubble wrap as a protection against rapid temperature plunges (see illustration 1). Fine-leaved plants and large containers will need a 3–5 cm (1–2 in) thick Hortag layer for drainage. The Hortag can be reused.
My tip: Buy some interlining fabric from a garden centre. Cut it to the size of the

2a Cutting slits in the basket liner.

2b Carefully planting through the slits.

container and lay it on the Hortag. This will avoid separating the drainage layer and compost in autumn.
● For plants that need large amounts of fertilizer, mix an extra portion of permanent fertilizer into the compost. This will save frequent feeding (see Types of fertilizer, p. 53).
● Fill each container with a layer of fresh compost (see Buying potting compost, p. 48).

Removing plants from their pots
Illustration 1

The relevant technique for this depends on the age and condition of the plant.

Older plants should be well watered. Wherever the roots have become entangled, use a long, clean knife to cut around the rootstock and prune away some of the old roots. This will also rejuvenate the plant, thereby increasing its vigour.
Matted rootstocks can be loosened carefully with fingers or cut off with a clean knife all the way around by about 1–2 cm (about 1 in).
Young plants generally fall readily out of plastic or clay pots.
All rootstocks grow better if they are well watered or soaked in a bowl before being repotted (see illustration 1).

2c A basket filled with colour-accord plants.

Repotting plants

● Arrange all the plant ingredients roughly in the new containers or boxes, placing trailing plants towards the front edge of the container, semi-erect ones in the centre, and erect and climbing ones at the back. Then remove the pots and plant up the new container, leaving enough space between each plant so that it has sufficient room to develop.
● Top up the container with compost to within 2.5 cm (1 in) of the rim, for watering.
● Firm the compost gently so the roots will quickly find contact with the compost.
● Water thoroughly.

My tip: Young plants will be very sensitive to sunlight during the first few days after planting. When necessary, cover them with newspaper.

Planting in hanging baskets
Illustration 2

Hanging baskets can be bought from garden centres and large DIY outlets.
● Secure the fixture to hold the basket in position before the basket is filled so that it can be hung as soon as it has been planted up (see Installing and overwintering containers, p. 54).
● Line the basket using moss or a piece of hessian for the outer layer. An inner layer of plastic will protect the plants from drying out.
● Create planting slits all round on two "levels" by cutting crosses in the liner (see illustration 2a).
● Fill the basket base with potting compost.
● Insert the roots of trailing plants for the bottom level through the slits (see illustration 2b). Then fill the basket with more compost.
● Plant the next level of slits with more trailers and add some more potting compost.
● Insert the semi-erect species from above.
● Add compost until the basket is almost full, firming it carefully.
● Water the basket thoroughly and hang it up (see illustration 2c).

Hydroculture
Illustration 3

Special containers for outdoor hydroculture can be used to water plants from a reservoir for up to two weeks. You can read off the moisture requirement from a water gauge. A controlled-release fertilizer ensures a sufficient supply of nutrients. The plants should be grown in a mixture of potting compost and Hortag, with some compost still adhering to their roots (see photo, p. 43; and illustration 3). When repotting in autumn, the Hortag can be separated and used again the following year. This eliminates some of the tiresome transportation of annual replacement materials. The containers used for outdoor hydroculture are also suitable for hardy woody plants.
Important: Young plants with small rootstocks should be watered regularly during the initial establishment period, until their roots are able to reach the nutrients in the pot.

3 Hydroculture: A cross-section of a pot.

Care & maintenance

The correct way to water

Profusely flowering balcony plants should be watered thoroughly as much moisture evaporates through the leaf surfaces.

● Freshly drawn water from the mains can cause a cold shock to plant roots. Stand the water in the sun for a while so it can warm up a little.

● Water directly onto the compost. Never spray the leaves as it encourages diseases.

● Water thoroughly between regular drying-out phases. If wet all the time, roots begin to rot.

● Water in the mornings in spring and autumn. In summer, water in the mornings and evenings – also at midday when the heat is great.

● Check containers of vigorous plants even in rainy weather, as their leaves may prevent the raindrops from penetrating the compost.

Watering during holidays

It is not always possible to look after plants every day. If you go away frequently, you will need to rely on helpful, trustworthy neighbours to do your watering, or you should use an automatic watering system, which can be expensive to install.

Hydroculture containers will provide water and nutrients for plants for about two weeks (see illustration 3, p. 51).

Water reservoirs in a false bottom in special boxes will supply water for about five days. A wick will draw water from the reservoir into the compost.

Ceramic cones in the compost are connected via a hose with a water tank or irrigation system.

When necessary, they will release water into the compost. *Computer-regulated watering systems* presuppose there is a supply of water and electricity to the balcony. An electrically controlled moisture "feeler" ensures that the right amount of water is transferred via a plastic pipe and drip hose.

Important: Before you leave, test whether the watering method functions properly.

Healthy balcony flowers give pleasure by blooming continuously.

Types of fertilizer

Many balcony plants have a high requirement of nutrients (see below). The potting compost alone will not cover these requirements. Vital additional minerals have to be supplied (see Buying potting compost, p. 18).

Compound fertilizers with a high proportion of phosphorus are suitable; these are generally labelled "flowering", "balcony flower" or "geranium" fertilizers. You should also obtain very good results with algae fertilizers, which do not leave a residue. These can be obtained in various forms:

Controlled-release granules can be mixed in with the compost before planting. At every watering, it will automatically release nutrients, so the plants will receive their optimal supply and will flower continuously. There is no need to repeat the fertilizing.

Fertilizer sticks are simply poked into the potting compost, and they usually last for six weeks. This can be relatively expensive if you have to feed numerous plants.

Liquid fertilizer should be mixed into the water. It is less expensive than fertilizer sticks but not as practical.

Important: Basic fertilizer in brand-name composts will not be sufficient for plants that are gross feeders. When planting these, add extra fertilizer at the time of potting (see The correct way to plant, p. 50).

Healthy balcony plants

Vigilant care will protect your plants from harmful insects and diseases, which attack weak, unhealthy plants. If you do see signs of any disease or pest, check whether the plants are being fed and watered correctly and are growing in suitable conditions for their needs (see The right position, p. 16). If you still find there are problems even when conditions seem optimal, seek expert advice on how to alleviate them.

Important: Make sure that any insecticides for flowering plants are not harmful to bees and other useful insects.

Plants' nutritional needs

Container plants fall into three planting groups depending on how much fertilizer they need.

Plants that require little fertilizer love to push their roots into meagre, nutrient-poor, loose soil or potting compost, and their readiness to bloom will rapidly decrease if they are given too much fertilizer.

Where a manufacturer's instructions gives different levels of doses, choose the lowest dose for these plants. If only one dose is mentioned, use half of it. Most wild flowers, cultivated plants with a wild character, many evergreen woody plants and shrubs prefer fairly small amounts of fertilizer. Usually they bear few flowers and leaves.

My tip: Overfertilizing robs many plants of their wonderful scent! Work with controlled-release fertilizer so that you do not accidentally give them too many nutrients.

Moderate feeders will be satisfied with a normal quantity of fertilizer. Most summer flowers, some shrubs and herbaceous plants as well as deciduous woody plants and bushes are moderate feeders.

Gross feeders have the highest requirements. Use the highest doses or double the quantity if only one level of dose is mentioned by a manufacturer.

Plants that have been highly developed as cultivars for the formation of large flowers and for endless flowering or fruiting – such as *Petunia* and geraniums – will consume vast quantities of fertilizer.

Installing and overwintering

Attachments for plant containers need to be suited to the size and weight of the container so that nobody will be injured by falling objects. When choosing the bracket or hook, bear in mind that plants get heavier as they grow and that wet compost weighs at least twice as much as dry compost.
Important: As there is always movement on a balcony, make sure that the containers stand firmly.

Attaching
Illustration 2

● Boxes can easily be secured to a railing with adjustable metal fixtures. A spacer will ensure that the box hangs straight. Wire frames are available for hanging up individual pots on a railing. Hang the containers on the inside of the balcony if they look too large, if you do not wish to create a safety risk or if the containers themselves are

intended to provide a decorative feature. The containers should be attached to the outside of the balcony if the balcony is rather small or if the plants are intended to decorate the facade of the house.
● You should be able to fix strong hooks for hanging baskets into the wall, into an overhead balcony or into the roofing (see illustration 2).
My tip: Attach your hanging baskets directly above the balcony boxes if possible. There, they will not take up much space and will serve as a "floating" visual screen.

Climbing aids
Illustrations 1 and 3

Perennial climbers are best used as an attractive visual screen or for flowering walls. If you would prefer annuals, choose vigorous plants that will quickly fulfil their task. You can attach **wires** or strings between a railing and the roof. Then plant

2 A hanging basket on a pulley for easy watering.

the climbers in the boxes and guide them up the wires (see illustration 3).
Trellis panels made of metal or wood can be bought from garden centres or large DIY outlets for free-standing displays or for fixing to a wall.
Mesh made of zinc-coated steel is a cheap alternative (see illustration 1). Ask the retailer to bend one end by 90 degrees for you. Stand the mesh in a box, fill it with potting compost and then plant up the box (see The correct way to plant, p. 50).

1 Climbers on rollers can provide a mobile visual screen on a balcony or patio.

3 A climbing framework of taut ropes.

My tip: Your visual screen for climbing plants can be mobile if you fix rollers under the boxes before planting them up (see illustration 1).

Overwintering

Most balcony plants are exhausted by autumn. Once they begin to look unsightly, throw them away. Some summer plants can be propagated from cuttings in late summer. Suitable plants include *Bidens ferulifolia*, geraniums, *Scaevola aemula*, *Petunia*, *Plectranthus* and *Glechoma hederacea*.

Taking cuttings: Cut an 8–10 cm (3–4 in) tip off a shoot just below a set of leaves; remove these leaves. Insert the shoot into some potting compost, which should be kept slightly moist.

Overwintering indoors

Perennials that are not hardy need to be overwintered indoors. *Evergreen* container plants like oleander, *Datura*, *Argyranthemum* and *Anisodontea capensis* should be cut back in late autumn and overwintered at 5–10°C (41–50°F). They should be placed in a bright position, particularly if there is no really cool room available.

Deciduous container plants like *Fuchsia*, *Cassia corymbosa* and pomegranate can be overwintered in a dark, cool place.

My tip: Ask a friend if you can overwinter any valuable and sensitive woody plants with high requirements of warmth and light – like citrus trees – in their heated greenhouse.

Water plants should be taken out of the water before the first frost. Empty the containers and allow them to dry. Plant the plants in a tub and overwinter them in a cool, frost-free, bright room. Water plants must never dry out.

Important: Check all your plants weekly in their winter quarters. Check roots are still slightly moist. Remove mouldy and dry leaves. Ventilate the room on frost-free days.

Overwintering outside
Illustration 4

Help hardy plants survive frosty days by introducing the following precautions.

Protect **root tips** from frost by wrapping the container with hessian sacking or bubble wrap, or inserting it between the compost and the container (see illustration 1, p. 50).

Large woody plants like roses, bamboos or perennial climbers are best covered with leaves and straw mats (see illustration 4). Protect **dwarf conifers** with spruce branches (see illustration 4).

Important: Frozen roots cannot absorb water. On sunny, frosty days evergreen plants may burn unless covered with hessian or rush matting.

4 Winter protection: straw mats and conifer branches.

English and botanical plant names

To help with your colour design, we have listed in this volume a host of wonderful balcony flowers with their botanical names as they are definite and internationally applicable. The following list gives the most common English equivalents.

Achnatherum calamagrostis feather grass
Acorus gramineus Japanese rush
Agrostemma githago corncockle
Ampelopsis ampelopsis
Anisodontea capensis anisodontea
Antirrhinum majus snapdragon
Argyranthemum frutescens argyranthemum
Asarina asarina
Asparagus asparagus
Aster aster
Bacopa water hyssop
Begonia begonia
Bellis perennis daisy
Bergenia cordifolia elephant's ears
Bidens ferulifolia bur marigold
Bougainvillea bouganivillea
Brachyscome multifida rock daisy
Briza quaking grass
Calceolaria integrifolia slipper flower
Callistephus chinensis China aster
Caltha pallustris marsh marigold
Campanula bellflower
Carex sedge
Caryopteris caryopteris
Cassia corymbosa cassia
Celosia cristata cockscomb

Centaurea cyanus cornflower
Centradenia centradenia
Chlorophytum chlorophytum
Cobaea scandens cathedral bell
Convolvulus sabatius bindweed
Convolvulus tricolor bindweed
Dahlia dahlia
Datura angels' trumpets
Dendranthema indicum chrysanthemum
Dianthus carnation, pink
Diascia vigilis diascia
Dicentra spectabilis bleeding heart
Eccremocarpus scaber Chilean glory flower
Erica gracilis heather
Eucomis comosa pineapple lily
Euphorbia spurge
Felicia amelloides Cape aster
Festuca gigantea giant fescue
Festuca scoparia fescue
Fragaria vesca wild strawberry
Fuchsia fuchsia
Gazania gazania
Glechoma hederacea ground ivy
Gomphrena gomphrena
Gypsophila repens gypsophila
Hedera helix common ivy

Helianthus annuus sunflower
Helichrysum helichrysum
Heliotropium arborescens heliotrope
Hosta hosta
Impatiens busy Lizzie
Ipomoea tricolor morning glory
Iris pseudacorus yellow flag
Juncus effusus rush
Juniperus juniper
Lagurus ovatus hare's tail
Lantana camara lantana
Lathyrus latifolius sweet pea
Lavandula angustifolia lavender
Lavatera olbia mallow
Limonium statice
Lobelia x speciosa lobelia
Lobularia maritima sweet alyssum
Lotus berthelotii parrot's beak
Malus apple
Melampodium paludosum melampodium
Mentha suaveolens apple mint
Moluccella laevis bells of Ireland
Muscari armeniacum grape hyacinth
Myosotis sylvatica forget-me-not
Nicotiana x sanderae tobacco plant
Nymphaea water lily
Nymphoides peltata water fringe
Origanum vulgare oregano
Osteospermum osteospermum
Papaver rhoeas Flanders poppy
Parthenocissus virginia creeper
Passiflora passion flower

Pelargonium geranium
Pennisetum orientale pennisetum
Pernettya pernettya
Petunia petunia
Phacelia scorpion weed
Phalaris arundinacea ribbon grass
Pharbitis acuminata pharbitis
Phaseolus coccineus runner bean
Phlox drummondii annual phlox
Plectranthus plectranthus
Pyracantha firethorn
Reseda odorata common mignonette
Rhodochiton atrosanguineus rhodochiton
Rosa rose
Rudbeckia hirta coneflower
Salvia sage
Sanvitalia procumbens creeping zinnia
Scaevola saligna scaevola
Sedum stonecrop
Silene coeli-rosa rose of heaven
Sinapis arvensis charlock
Skimmia japonica skimmia
Solanum jasminoides potato vine
Solanum rantonnetii blue potato bush
Spartina michauxiana prairie cord grass
Sutera sutera
Tagetes tagetes
Thunbergia alata black-eyed Susan
Tropaeolum majus nasturtium
Tulipa tulip
Typha minima bulrush
Verbena verbena
Viola pansy, violet
Vitis vinifera grapevine
Zinnia zinnia

Petunia play the main part in this atmospheric flowering display.

Index

Author's notes

This volume deals with the colourful design of balcony plants. When repotting large plants (see The correct way to plant, p. 50), the leaves or branches in particular may injure the eyes. It is therefore a good idea to wear protective gloves and goggles while doing jobs around such plants. If you sustain an injury, visit your doctor to discuss the possibility of having a tetanus vaccination. When working on a balcony make sure you do not get into situations where you might suffer an attack of vertigo, and always keep your feet on a firm base, particularly when using a ladder. Some of the plants described here may be toxic and may cause considerable problems to frail adults or children. Before purchasing plants, get information on their toxicity and make absolutely sure that children and domestic pets do not eat the poisonous parts. Always check that the additional weight on a balcony from furnishings and large planted containers does not exceed 250 kg per square meter (55 lb per square foot). All pots, containers, boxes and hanging baskets must be fixed securely and safely according to specifications (see Installing and overwintering, p. 54). All fertilizers and plant protection agents, even organic ones, should be stored according to the directions on the packet and in such a way that they are inaccessible to children and domestic pets. Consumption of these agents may damage health. They should not be allowed to come into contact with your eyes. Take note of all safely precautions on the packaging.

The meanings of the seasonal indicator abbreviations used on pp. 21–45 are as follows:

ESP	= early spring
MSP	= mid-spring
LSP	= late spring
ES	= early summer
MS	= mid-summer
LS	= late summer
EA	= early autumn
MA	= mid-autumn
LA	= late autumn
EW	= early winter
MW	= mid-winter
LW	= late winter

Acknowledgements

All photographs in this volume are by Friedrich Strauss except cover photographs by L. Rose.

The author and publishers would like to thank the artist Siegbert Hahn of Cologne for his artistic advice.

Cover photographs

Front cover: *Petunias; marigold dwarf-crested French series; Rosa 'Cristata'; phlox.*
Inside front cover: *A cheerful, colourful group.*
Back cover: *Nasturtiums.*

This edition published 1998 by Merehurst Limited
Ferry House
51–57 Lacy Road
Putney
London SW15 1PR

© 1997 Gräfe und Unzer GmbH, Munich

ISBN 1 85391 674 9

A catalogue record for this book is available from the British Library.

English text copyright © Merehurst Limited 1998
Translated by Astrid Mick
Edited and typeset by Joanna Chisholm
Printed in Hong Kong by Wing King Tong.

Variations in the autumn

When winter is not far off and autumnal mists envelope the plants in a veil, an arrangement with subdued mixed colours is particularly beautiful. You will find colour mixtures in red, blue and white in varying proportions on this enchanting patio. The umbels of *Sedum spectabile* in charming mauve, the pink and violet flowers of asters and the blue-violet bells of *Campanula rapunculoides* together form a colour run. The foliage is covered with a matt sheen as if it had already caught the first hoar frost. The flat light underlines the multiple structures of the plants.

The plants in this enchanting autumnal design cover the whole colour spectrum from pink to blue-violet.